by Noah Leatherland

Bearport Books, an imprint of Bearport Publishing by FlutterBee

Credits
All images are courtesy of Shutterstock.com, unless otherwise specified. With thanks to Getty Images, Thinkstock Photo, and iStockphoto.

Cover and title page, © Grzegorz Czapski, Dong liu, Supermop, Calreyn88, CC0 via Wikimedia Common; Background pattern throughout, © topform; 2–3, © auto-data.net; 4–5, © Gorodenkoff, betto rodrigues; 6–7, © auto-data.net, Markus Wissmann; 8–9, © Jack Skeens, VanderWolf Images; 10–11, © slava296, Alexandre Prevot; 12–13, © Sport car hub, Mike Mareen; 14–15, © Ethan Yetman, Alexandros Michailidis; 16–17, © Sam Moores, Mike Mareen, Khairil Azhar Junos; 18–19, © 1933 Media Productions, phjahn; 20–21, © Gabo_Arts; 22–23, © Erik Cox Photography, Ethan Yetman

Bearport Publishing Company Product Development Team
Kayla Eggert, Theresa Emminizer, Kim Jones, Allison Juda, Cole Nelson, Naomi Reich, Steve Scheluchin, Tiana Tran

Library of Congress Cataloging-in-Publication Data is available at www.loc.gov or upon request from the publisher.

ISBN: 979-8-89577-606-3 (hardcover)
ISBN: 979-8-89577-694-0 (ebook)

For more information, write to Bearport Publishing, 3500 American Blvd W, Suite 150, Bloomington, MN 55431.
Printed in the United States of America.

CONTENTS

FAST CARS

Fast, powerful cars make for a thrilling ride. Let's take a look at some truly extreme cars. How speedy do they get?

PAGANI HUAYRA

MODEL YEAR: **2011** FROM: **Italy**

In about 3 seconds, this car can go from 0 to 60 miles per hour (100 kph).

The Pagani Huayra is named after Huayra Tata—the **ancient** South American god of wind. Two **turbochargers** power the car to go superfast, allowing the vehicle to reach a top speed of 238 mph (383 kph)!

01

SPEED SCORE

4

ASPARK OWL

MODEL YEAR: **2023** FROM: **Japan**

Electric cars can help the **environment** *and* give you a rush of excitement at the same time! With max speeds of up to 273 mph (439 kph), the Aspark Owl has set world records as one of the fastest electric cars ever made.

There are only 50 Aspark Owls in the world.

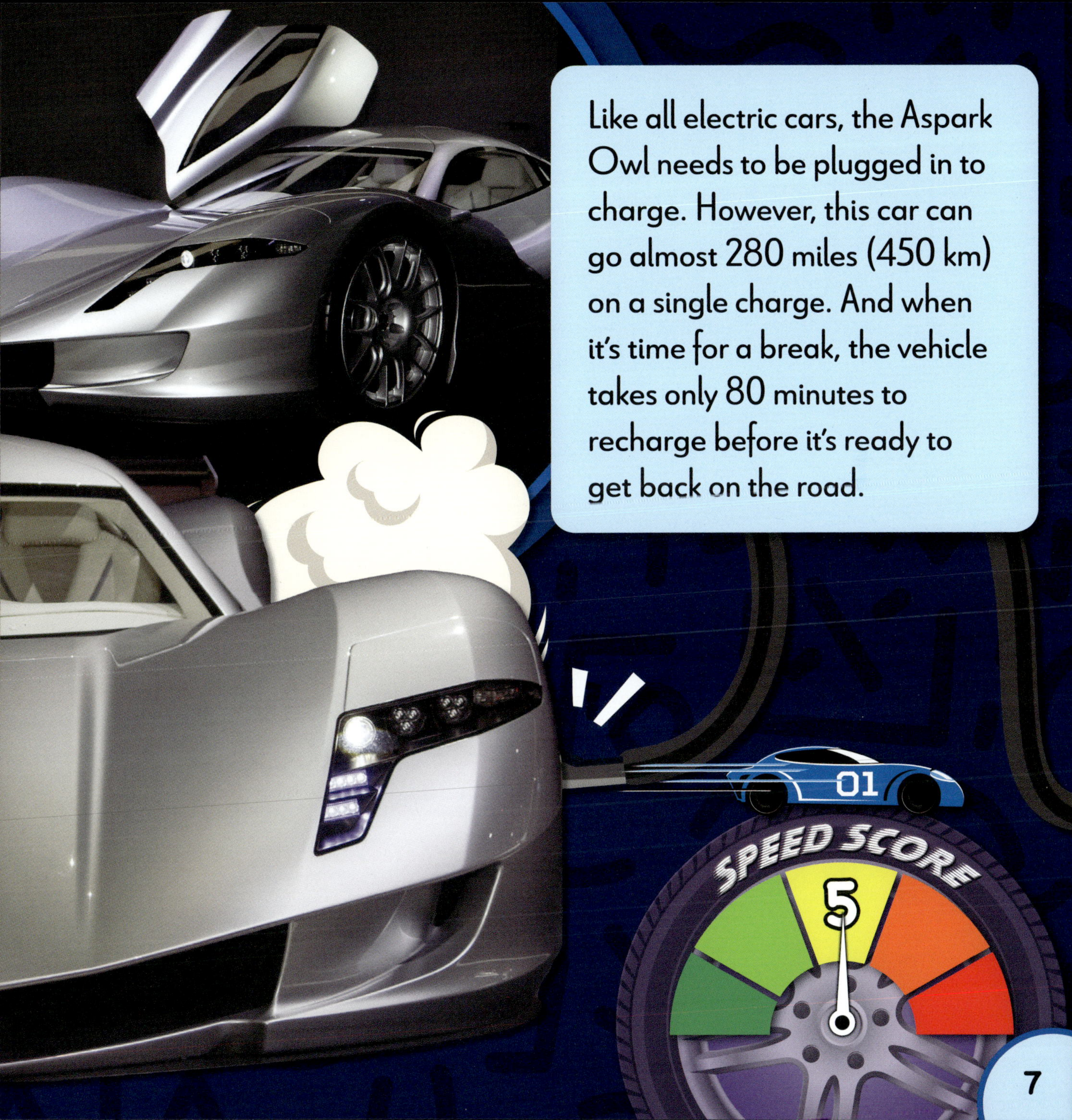

Like all electric cars, the Aspark Owl needs to be plugged in to charge. However, this car can go almost 280 miles (450 km) on a single charge. And when it's time for a break, the vehicle takes only 80 minutes to recharge before it's ready to get back on the road.

KOENIGSEGG REGERA

MODEL YEAR: **2015** FROM: **Sweden**

The Koenigsegg Regera is often called a megacar. Why? Because of its 1,500 **horsepower** engine. This **hybrid engine** includes twin turbochargers and three electric **motors**.

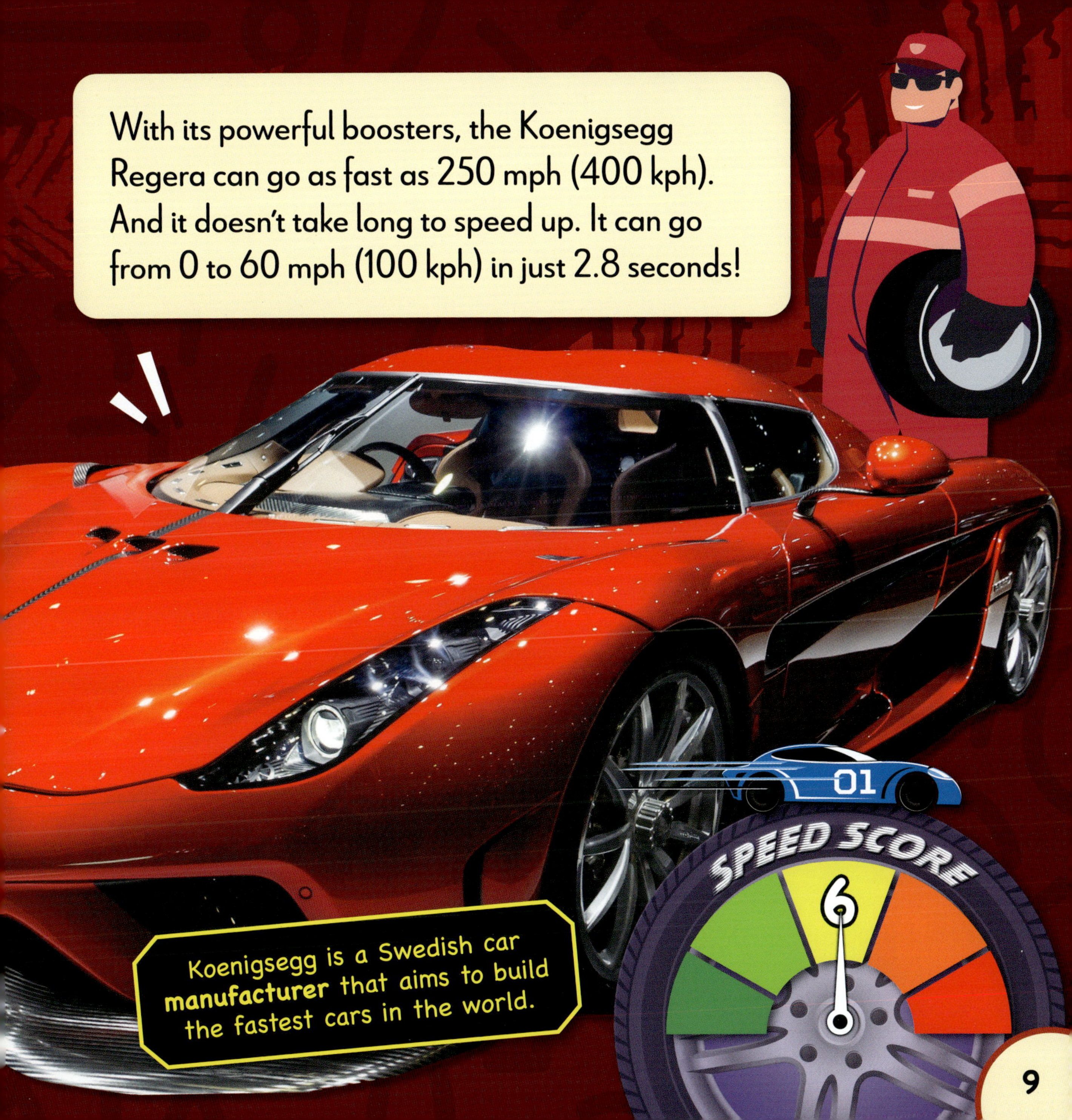
With its powerful boosters, the Koenigsegg Regera can go as fast as 250 mph (400 kph). And it doesn't take long to speed up. It can go from 0 to 60 mph (100 kph) in just 2.8 seconds!
Koenigsegg is a Swedish car **manufacturer** that aims to build the fastest cars in the world.
01
SPEED SCORE
6

ASTON MARTIN VALKYRIE

MODEL YEAR: **2021** FROM: **United Kingdom**

The British car manufacturer Aston Martin was **inspired** by some of the most famous race cars in history. They wanted to make vehicles that could hit superhigh speeds off the tracks, too. So, they built the Valkyrie.

The Valkyrie's license plate holder contains a first aid kit.

With 1,139 horsepower, this car has lots of power while still fitting into tight city spaces. It can also take corners at superfast speeds.
01
SPEED SCORE
6
412Y

MCLAREN SPEEDTAIL

MODEL YEAR: **2018** FROM: **United Kingdom**

McLaren is a manufacturer known for its superfast cars.

The McLaren Speedtail looks like it came racing in from the future. It was tested at the Kennedy Space Center in Florida. There, it reached a speed of 250 mph (400 kph). No wonder they call it the Speedtail!

What makes the Speedtail so extreme? It is teardrop shaped, which creates less drag to help the car move fast. The Speedtail is also very light for a car, weighing just 3,150 pounds (1,430 kg).

RIMAC NEVERA

MODEL YEAR: **2021** FROM: **Croatia**

Meet the all-electric car that beat 23 world records in a single day. It's the Rimac Nevera! With four electric motors, this car's engine packs more than 1,900 horsepower.

There are only 150 Rimac Neveras in the world.

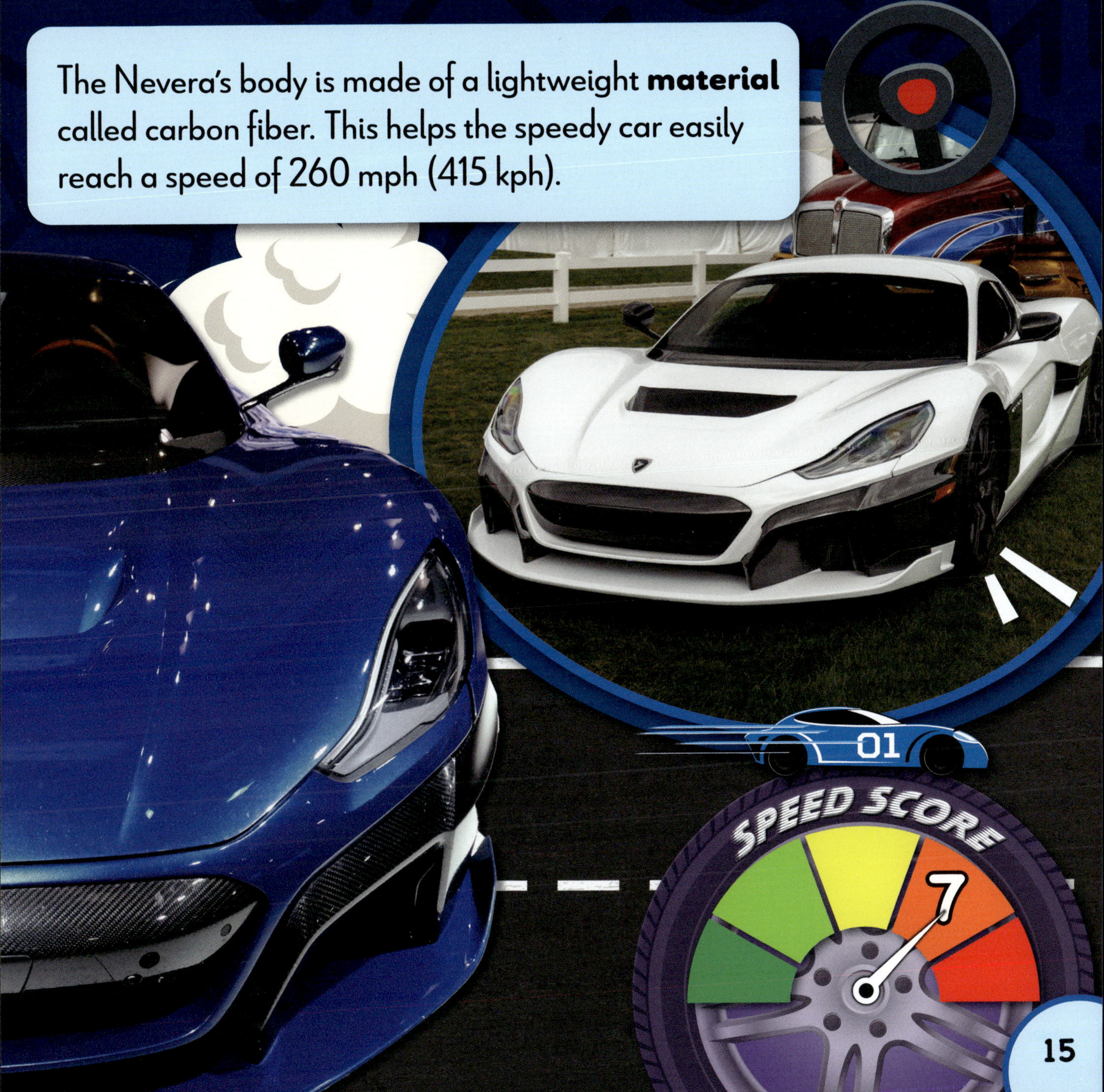

The Nevera's body is made of a lightweight **material** called carbon fiber. This helps the speedy car easily reach a speed of 260 mph (415 kph).

SSC TUATARA

MODEL YEAR: **2021** FROM: **United States**

The SSC Tuatara comes from a long line of superfast American cars. It was SSC's latest attempt at making the fastest car in the world.

Recording the Tuatara's top speed took a few tries. This car went through several mechanical difficulties, including losing power mid-test run. However, it is now said to have an incredible top speed of 296 mph (476 kph)!

BUGATTI CHIRON

MODEL YEAR: **2021** FROM: **France**

The Bugatti Chiron Super Sport 300+ is the first sports car to ever go faster than 300 mph (483 kph). That's how it got its name!

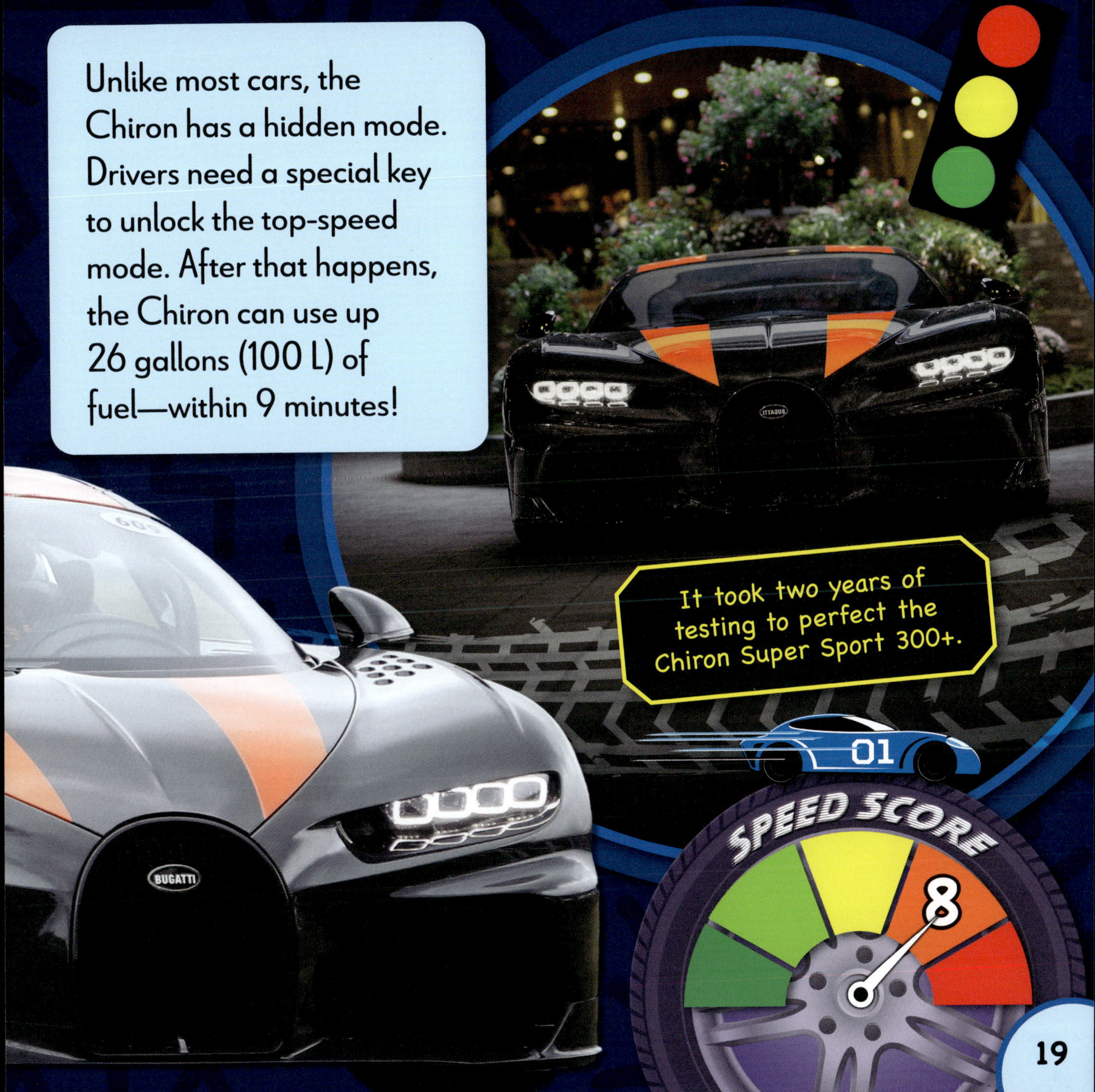
Unlike most cars, the Chiron has a hidden mode. Drivers need a special key to unlock the top-speed mode. After that happens, the Chiron can use up 26 gallons (100 L) of fuel—within 9 minutes!
It took two years of testing to perfect the Chiron Super Sport 300+.
01
SPEED SCORE
8
BUGATTI

HENNESSEY VENOM F5

MODEL YEAR: **2022** FROM: **United States**

Hennessey manufacturers were first known for **modifying** other cars to make them faster. Later, they started to build their own cars from scratch.

With a top speed of 272 mph (438 kph), the Hennessey Venom F5 is their fastest car yet. And the company isn't stopping there. Its engineers are working hard to make the car crack 310 mph (500 kph).

The Venom F5 has a horsepower of 1,817!

KOENIGSEGG JESKO ABSOLUT

MODEL YEAR: **2022** FROM: **Sweden**

What is the fastest car in the world? Well, in theory, it's Koenigsegg's Jesko Absolut. It just hasn't been proven . . . yet. Engineers are still testing the Jesko Absolut's true limits, but they say it can go more than 310 mph (500 kph)!

The body of the Jesko Absolut is made for air to easily glide over it.

To do this, the Jesko Absolut is powered by twin-turbos with 1,600 horsepower. Its rear is inspired by fighter jets, which helps the car travel faster.

GLOSSARY

ancient belonging to a long time ago

environment the natural world where plants, animals, and people live

horsepower a measure of an engine's power based on how many horses it would take to do the same work

hybrid engine an engine that uses both electricity and liquid fuel

inspired given the idea to do something

manufacturer a person or company that makes things to sell

material a thing from which objects are made

modifying changing in some way

motors machines that use power to make things move or work

turbochargers devices that are powered by exhaust gases to spin a specific part in the car

INDEX